FROM THE AUTHOR OF *PRACTICE OF THE PRACTICE*

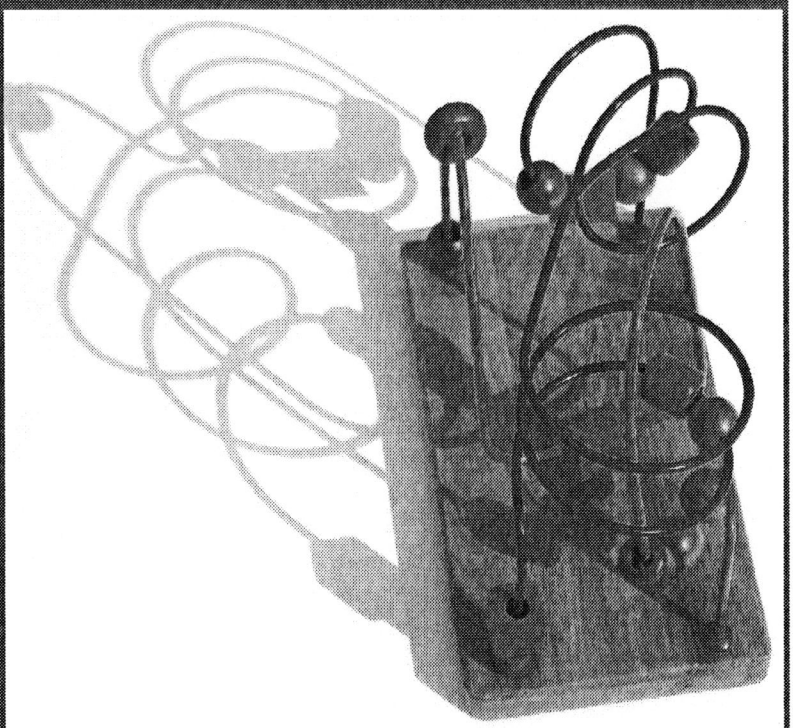

MENTAL
WELLNESS
PARENTING

A REMARKABLY SIMPLE APPROACH
TO MAKING PARENTING EASIER

JOSEPH R. SANOK, MA

LICENSED PROFESSIONAL COUNSELOR | LIMITED LICENSED PSYCHOLOGIST
NATIONAL CERTIFIED COUNSELOR | FATHER | HUSBAND

Mental Wellness Parenting

A remarkably simple approach to making parenting easier

JOSEPH R. SANOK

Mental Wellness Counseling | A remarkably simple approach to making parenting easier is a work of nonfiction. Nonetheless, some of the names and personal characteristics of individuals or events have been changed in order to disguise identities. Any resulting resemblance to persons, living or dead is entirely coincidental and unintentional.

Copyright © 2012 by Joseph R. Sanok

All rights reserved.

Published in the United States by Sanok Counseling PLLC, Traverse City, MI.

www.mentalwellnesscounseling.com

First Edition

Edited and feedback given by Jessica Doerr. Thanks!

Book cover design by Joseph R. Sanok

Cover photography by Aaron VanHeest

Other books by Joseph R. Sanok

Practice of the Practice | A Start-up Guide to Launching a Private Practice

The Ten-minute Toddler Turnaround | Improving Sleep

For Rick and MaryEllen, my parents. Thanks for all the sticker charts and my first sword.

Thanks for being great examples.

I love you!

Legal Stuff

This publication is designed to provide accurate and authoritative information in regard to the subject matter covered. It is provided with the understanding that the author and publisher are not engaged in rendering legal, accounting, counseling, or other professional services. If legal advice or other expert assistance is required, the service of a competent professional person should be sought.

All names in this book are changed, as well as identifying features so as to align with HIPAA and FERPA and protect the client's identity.

Also, please don't copy this book illegally.

TABLE OF CONTENTS

Introduction..17

Keep the Change..27

Pain Motivates..37

Good Soup..41

Control vs. Voice..47

Big dates, first days of school, and tickets.............59

Purpose?..77

Life tips that apply to parenting.........................87

Quick Topic Lists...113

Now What?...129

Resources...133

Welcome!

This all started when I wouldn't go to bed. I wanted to watch the train go by our house and stay up for Fraggle Rock. I was four. My father, a psychologist, and my mother, a nurse, knew that sleep was tied to brain development and behavior. Also I'm sure they wanted some alone time. They started a sticker chart for me to "earn something from the store."

I didn't know what the "something" was, but as a four-year-old, I had no means to get anything. I gained a sense of power and control over my situation. When the day finally came, my father took me to the grocery store. I didn't even know my options. Then he said, "What about a sword? Every boy needs a sword."

Of course, clearly every boy does need a sword. The primary male in my life was telling me that this was something a boy needed. I was a boy, he was a man, he must know, so of course I then wanted it.

It was that, the first moment of mindful positive reinforcement that started my parents on a path of clear expectations, consequences, and behavioral ups and downs.

A sword frames my story. Really it is not the sword, but the sticker habit that guided my behavior.

Whether you are launching or improving your parenting, this e-book will help you get to the next level. Also, there is a whole community of parents, professionals, and learners that are engaging deeper through the Mental Wellness Parenting Facebook Page, will you join the discussion?

Thanks for joining me in the journey.

If you have questions, let's talk:

Joe

December 2012
Traverse City
joe@mentalwellnesscounseling.com

INTRODUCTION

Less text and more action.

You don't have time to read a bunch of fluff, you're a parent.

Get in and get out that is what I think.

I want these ideas to motivate you so that you set the book down and try them immediately. If you read this book straight through, I have failed.

I don't want to fail.

Quick, think of the most annoying behavior that your child does.

What is it? (write it here)

Mental Wellness Parenting

I hate when my child does...

How do you know when this is happening?

The very first thing you must learn is to accurately discuss and identify your kid's behavior. We'll get more into this, but start thinking about it now.

These types of exercises and quick thoughts are how we're going to fly through a remarkably simple approach to making parenting easier.

That's my bottom line: PARENTING DOES NOT HAVE TO BE AS HARD AS IT IS!

Introduction

That's what we're about to do. It's like a brief counseling session where you come in, we talk about what's going on and then you run out of the office, excited to test out what you've just learned. Not years of therapy, but short and focused sessions to motivate you toward action.

If I talk too much, then skip ahead. Here are a few things that I think you should know. It's a quick overview of why you should trust me with your parenting and your kids and my basic philosophy. **If you are in a hurry or just ready to get going, jump to where it says "To summarize."**

I have long wanted to write a book about parenting. I began working with "at-risk" youth in 1998 when I was completing my Bachelor's degree in psychology. I worked in numerous job settings: a short-term residential facility, court-mandated programs, and a Boys & Girls Club. When I earned my Masters degrees in Counseling Psychology and Community Counseling, I saw the same themes develop. I have worked with kids and families in foster care, college settings, and at my private practice Mental Wellness Counseling.

Over and over, students were wholly blamed for their behaviors. Of course each of us has a choice in how we live our lives, but it is also substantially easier to follow the direction that we have experienced. How often have you said to yourself, "I sound just like my mother"?

Like water, the path of least resistance is usually what we take. My mother did it this way, so it is natural that I will follow those basics. You may tweak exactly what that looks like, but the general concepts are usually quite similar.

But it doesn't have to be that way.

You can reform, revolutionize, and transform your parenting.

You can be completely different from where you came from.

Introduction

Like water, though, something needs to change in your environment. If a stream flows it will continue to flow unless the environment changes. As it cools, ice builds around the edges and water can take a completely different path. As it warms, it may move into a fog, cloud, travel to Germany, fall down as snow in Switzerland, and then melt in the mountain lakes.

Water changes when something outside of itself changes, but it still remains the same element. It is the same with each of us. We often need that extra push, the heat or cooling, to take us out of the stream that we have floated down our entire lives.

Now is the time to decide to be a better parent and form new habits so that you create a different stream.

This book will help you in multiple ways. It is meant to be both cumulative and singular. By that I mean that as a whole it tells a story and gives a framework that builds upon itself. Therefore, the cumulative work can help you transform your parenting.

It is also singular in that it you can pick up any chapter and gain something from it. As a busy parent, you may just need a quick idea or a spark to help you think differently.

These are two different approaches, but they both have value. I'm glad that you are starting this process.

If you do plan on reading the entire book as a cumulative work, here are some tips that I believe will help.

First, people crave community. Alcoholics Anonymous has been highly successful because of their focus on creating a new community for people that need to shift their lives. I recommend that you find someone to read this book with.

Maybe your best friend and you often lament about parenting. Commit to read a chapter a week and then discuss how you will implement it. Or maybe a group from your church wants to study it and then have

Introduction

follow-up meetings to discuss how you're continuing to form a new parenting path.

When I read a book, I always have this idea that I will retain the information and know where the great points are. I have come to realize that although I think this about myself, it just is not true. So I underline, star, and number things. What I do is I circle definitions I like. I number points that are made. Things that I really like I put a star or arrows next to it. At the end of every book I read, I will write profound thoughts that I have or actions that I want to take. I do it at the end of the book rather than a journal, because then I can put the page numbers that spurred on that thought.

When I go back and review a book, it is much easier to find what I'm looking for. Also, when I read my notes at the end, I am always amazed at the thoughts I had, but how they seem to have disappeared deep into my subconscious.

Lastly, as parents we have crazy lives. There is always something going on that competes for our attention. Laundry, food, soccer, and daily tasks can pile up and drive us crazy. Changing your parenting style is going to take work.

While you read this book, figure out some way to set aside time outside of the house. Really look at your schedule and see where you can steal 15-30 minutes a week. Maybe while you're waiting to pick up your child you turn off the radio and pull out the book. Things will distract you away from making these changes.

In the long run, it will actually save you time. As your children's behavior improves, your mental health and time will grow.

You can do it! Remember, these are just words, but you will use them to move from a flowing river to a completely new path.

To summarize: What this book is and is not.
When you are finished with this book, you will not be a better parent. Contrary to popular belief, books and

Introduction

knowledge do nothing. Rather, you need to take these ideas and words and concepts and in some way implement them.

You can do this in a number of ways:

1. **Set down the book every time you have an idea or read it quickly first:** Read through the book quickly to get an overview, skim the pictures, graphs, bold, and main points (if you're like me, you've already done this).

2. **Don't do it alone:** Find someone that will join you in this journey. Find another Dad that wants to become a better father. Ask a group from church to join you in reading this. Call a friend in Wisconsin and ask them to read it with you, and then talk weekly.

3. **Read through it and take notes:** Here are some suggestions:

    Highlight only things that you want to do immediately (maybe color code by your children, if one idea is good for Billy and another is good for Lydia, use different highlighters)

Star items that are really good ideas.

Put a question make by things you want to discuss with someone.

<u>Underline</u> main points

Write comments on the side

KEEP THE CHANGE

I wouldn't be a counselor if I didn't think that counseling was a good idea. It's not in my personality to do things that I don't find right. So if I felt I was suckering people, I couldn't live with the guilt.

With that said, I don't think that counseling is for everyone.

I hope that this book gives you a peek into sessions with me so that you can learn from my experiences and what I tell clients.

WHY THERAPY IS BETTER

In therapy, there are three things that are achieved:

1. Accountability
2. Insight
3. Tweaking

Let me tell you what I mean.

In order for therapy to work, the client has to show up. Usually, not only do they have to do that, but they also have to think about issues and discussions outside of the session. I usually start with a statement: "Tell me what you've been working on." "What went well this week?" or "Where should we start?"

This is an intentional beginning that forces most clients to reflect on their progress. They have someone that is asking them:

"Why are things still the same?"

"Shouldn't you be working harder on these things?"

Secondly, clients get real-time insight. We discuss issues they often verbally process until they get around to their point, and then finally see that why they came in is not why they came in. Somewhere in their search for words, they found what is really behind their hurt, depression, or inability to make love to their partner. Insight, whether in their own processing or in a bit of advice or perspective, pushes them forward.

Lastly, we have tweaking. I love the word "tweak." For one, it sounds light-hearted. It grows on you the more you use it. Within "tweak" is the idea that you're pretty much on track, but just stepping a touch in the wrong direction. By "tweaking" how clients approached a situation we improve future outcomes.

Accountability, insight, and tweaking all come from a counseling session...well, most sessions, sometimes I am a bit off.

APPROACHING THIS BOOK LIKE A COUNSELING SESSION

Now that you know my big secret, you can approach this book and really your whole life, as a counseling session. Let's examine these three items again.

ACCORDING TO ACCOUNTABILITY

According to the US Census (http://www.census.gov/population/www/pop-profile/geomob.html) one out of every six people will move this year. Each of us moves around 11.7 times in our lifetime. This is significantly different from previous generations, where grandparents knew kids and they all stayed in the same communities.

What we lost from that old structure was a sense of community and accountability. People can get divorced and the neighbors don't talk, because they have not met the couple. Kids start using drugs and go into rehab and start listening to music that drives their parents crazy, yet grandma can't check in on the teen because he's across the country.

Building accountability in our lives helps us reach our goals and stay on track, even as we move.

When I was in college, I went to a church that encouraged college students to have "accountability partners." Those accountability partners were meant to help each other make good decisions, have deeper conversations, and keep growing.

I believe that the concept is universally true that when we have people to check in with us, we tend to work towards out goals.

INSIGHT

The second area of counseling is insight. In sessions, insight usually comes in two forms, from within the person and from outside of the person. More often than not, my role is to help people discover what is already inside them. Usually they have overcome a similar experience and just need to recognize those skills and apply them to a new situation.

When someone learns to see their skills and strengths from previous situations, then apply them to new areas, that skill can be expanded upon indefinitely.

The other area of insight is from outside of them. Usually this happens when I provide new information. Part of why the process moves quicker in therapy than outside of life is because the client both trusts my judgment and also is expecting change. When we have someone that can weed through the crazy theories of life and say, "Give this one a whirl" it is easier. This is especially true over time. When someone has success with one of my recommendations, they trust future judgments more often.

Further, a client comes to counseling because they expect change. That expectation alone can often expand anything that I say, because the person wants to be successful.

Thus, in applying this book as a therapy session, you have to find how to have both internal and external insight.

Internal insight comes from journaling, challenging previous thoughts, and applying your strengths to new situations.

Keep the Change

External insight comes from finding sources that you trust to help siphon through the flood of information that is available.

As well, you have to expect change to happen.

TWEAKING

The last area of bringing counseling session principles into your life without paying $150+ an hour...tweaking. What needs tweaking? How do you get that feedback loop? When your spouse/partner tells you something needs "tweaking," how do you react? What emotions does it bring out? Why?

Aren't they trying to tell you what would help them be more happy and how to improve things between you?

There are certain people that can't help me tweak, I might call them **anti-tweak people**. Usually, family members, long-time friends, and especially siblings...I have a hard time hearing anything that remotely sounds like "tweaking." I have tweak earmuffs for those situations. Also, I might have tweak goggles, or even a tweak bag to put over my head. With them I am anti-tweak.

I know it is not right, because they are closest to me and probably have deep insights that would help me.

We all have those people that make us feel anti-tweak and it is unhealthy.
Those are the people that we need to most listen to. They know us. They don't say it in a nice way, they say it in a straight-forward way. To us it is not a tweak, it is an adjustment or change or "What were you thinking when you did that!"...but we still need to hear it.

So who is going to hold you accountable? How are you going to build internal and external insight? How will you learn to tweak?

Keep the Change

To summarize:

1. **You need accountability to follow this book, find someone!**
2. **Expect change and insight.**
3. **Tweak what you try in small steps.**

PAIN MOTIVATES

Pain has a way of motivating us. When we're in the midst of heartache or change, we want nothing more than to remove it from our lives. We want to ensure that it never returns. We hope that when we change, we'll never again get divorced, our kids won't get angry like they once did, or that friendships won't fall apart.

Pain is a motivator because we want a sense of control. By "pain" I mean the potential for or actual feels of pain. For example, when I was diagnosed with cancer, I felt completely helpless. At first, I didn't want to think about it. I didn't want to learn more or study or research, I just wanted to ignore it. I was in disbelief.

Then something changed, everything changed.

It was right before my surgery. I felt power over my situation through acquiring knowledge. I learned what

I could control to reduce the likelihood of cancer returning and also learned what was completely out of

my hands. My diet shifted and slowly so did many of my unhealthy attitudes.

Pain is a motivator.

But it is not that way with kids. Pain is a motivator for us because we have abilities to change our situations. We can read, learn, and talk with our support network. We can go out into the world and shift our outcomes. Kids have not acquired those skills and often don't have the power to freely stand up against what is causing them pain.

Depending on their age, they may not even be able to articulate what is causing anxiety, pain, and worry. Think about the complexity of what we do naturally.

As adults we have pain. We identify what the source of the pain is. We evaluate what we can do to reduce that pain. We then assess our own abilities to reduce what

Pain Motivates

is happening. Then we identify where we can get new skills, knowledge, and outcomes. We evaluate the options and then select what we think is best. After that we follow those steps, we read books, join support groups, go to counseling…all of this takes skills of finding information, talking to new people, and having access to phones/email/computer/books. We then take what we have learned and implement those changes to reduce our pain, at least the portion that we have control of.

It is a very complex process to reduce our pain.

It is no wonder that kids get anxious. They experience pain, hurt, and heartache just like us, yet they rarely have any sense of true control over their situation.

Then, on top of all that, the adults in their lives tell them to "get over it" or to "handle it like a big boy or girl," yet they don't know what that even means.

This is where our discussion begins. How do we talk to our kids? First, we need to learn to discuss what is happening and break it down into easy to understand bits. Next, we need to remember that kids are more motivated by moving toward something positive than avoiding something negative.

To summarize:

1. **Pain motivates adults to want to change their situation.**
2. **This process is highly complex and kids have a hard time doing part or all of it.**
3. **Kids need guides to accurately help them learn behavior through clear discussions and working toward something positive.**

GOOD SOUP

Being a good parent is like making soup. For those of you who have never made soup, except out of a can I'm sorry. You are truly missing out.

When making a good soup you can of course follow a recipe. But, some of the greatest surprises are when you create a soup from what you have and then it is amazing. As you sip that steamy amazing broth and dip bread to absorb the flavor, you understand that you may never taste this exact soup again. You savor it. When it is gone, you attempt to replicate it, but only if you are lucky will you create the exact same flavor again.

When I make soup, I look in the fridge and review what we have and need to get rid of. If we're lacking, I move toward the freezer. I may start with sautéing meat or onions, then I'll add additional vegetables to create a depth of flavor. I may add some flour to the oil or butter to make a roux.

When I was volunteering in New Orleans at a shelter for people in the final stages of AIDS, I asked a number of the nurses, "Can I have your gumbo recipe?" They almost always replied, "Son, you just use whatcha got in da fridge, or you use Zataran's."

I had no working knowledge of the base of gumbo, how could I just throw things in? So I took a Cajun cooking class with some of the residents. I learned the basics of building flavor in a roux then adding onion, green pepper, and celery (the "holy trinity"), rice, and stock. From there, you add whatever you want sausage, turkey, chicken, shellfish, shrimp, or veggies that are about to go bad.

BUILDING THE ROUX OF PARENTING

Parenting is the same as making a good gumbo or soup, you have to acquire a basic understanding of guiding principles. Once these are gained, your soup/children will usually turn out pretty darn good. Once you gain the flavors that build to a solid adult, you can start thinking differently about what you are teaching your kids.

HOW DO WE DEFINE BE A "SUCCESSFUL ADULT"?

We all define "success" differently. Where I went to school in Michigan, everyone was expected to go to college. But why did parents value that over other things? To those parents, college represented being able to provide for yourself and have a career and standard of living that was more comfortable.

Is that what we should teach our kids, to be comfortable?

No, but I think the guiding idea was even deeper. The world is full of opportunities and challenges. Some of us are dealt better hands than others, but when we do something there is almost always a reaction that occurs. Some call this a "consequence", others call this a "reward" or "punishment", others call this a "speeding ticket."

When we really look at the "roux" of life, when we do things there are almost always consequences, both positive and negative.

HOW DO WE TEACH IT?

The more that we can outline natural consequences for decisions and let our children succeed or fail, the more they can learn those connections. The part of the brain (the frontal lobe) that connects behavior and consequence, does not fully develop in more adults until around age 22. Some newer research is showing that it may be even later. Thus, kids often need a parent's help, even in college, connecting what they have done and what occurred as a result of it. Thus statements like...

They should know better.

Act your age.

Grow up and just do it.

...aren't very helpful. Rather, describing children's behavior helps them to identify what worked and did not work.

FAILURE BUILDS CONFIDENCE

Of course we don't seek out to make our kids fail. However, we often seek to shield them from failure. To allow our kids to fail goes against our basic instinct of protection and safety. In our self-esteem-driven culture, a sense of entitlement has permeated kid's and parent's attitudes. When a child fails a test, the teacher is often blamed, rather than the child or parent. Working with your child to grow their own personal responsibility and experience appropriate failure will help them feel more in control. As they learn their own ability to make the world more how they want it, they will actually think more carefully about age-appropriate decisions.

Further, it allows the parent to step back and be more of a guide than a monitor.

Our remarkably simple approach to making parenting easier holds all of these elements in balance. We'll go more in detail but it's all in the roux of parenting.

With these basic building-blocks of parenting, you can try all sorts of new recipes for your own parenting soup.

To summarize:

1. **With basic building blocks, parenting will be remarkably easy.**
2. **Define success first, what is being an adult?**
3. **Teach through being specific and clear.**
4. **Appropriate failure builds confidence.**

CONTROL VS. VOICE

So how do we use this new information about guiding our kids to help them change their behavior? Ultimately, you have no control over your child. They make decisions every day. They are their own persons.

Webster's defines "control" as: "To exercise restraining or directing influence over. To have power over. Reduce the incidence or severity of especially to innocuous levels <control an insect population> <control a disease>"

The part of this definition that I like is the "directing influence over". I would argue that this comes less from control and more from having a voice in your child's life.

One of Webster's definitions of "voice" is, "wish, choice, or opinion openly or formally expressed." So to have a "voice" in your child's life is for your wishes, choices, and opinions to somehow take root in them.

hink about who has a voice in your life. Who can say to you, "Here is my opinion" and you consider it?

Is it your mom?

Dad?

Best friend?

Wife or husband or significant other?

How did they gain that voice in your life? Did they do something? Did they act a certain way? Is it because you have seen how they live their life and you respect that? Do you aspire to be like them or certain parts of them? What is it that allows them to have that voice, not control, in your life?

I believe that it is trust. They somehow built trust in you. Building a voice comes from trust. For kids, that trust comes from three specific things. To build trust as parents we must demonstrate:

1. Consistency and love
2. Set an example
3. Spur something in our children that brings life

CONSISTENCY AND LOVE

In future chapters I will discuss more in-depth what this looks like and ways that you can increase consistency and demonstrate your love. One definition of "consistency" is "agreement or harmony of parts or features to one another or a whole."

To be a consistent parent, you have to have harmony in what you do. What does this mean? It means that it is better to say nothing at all, rather than a false promise. By false promise I mean not following through on things you say. If you give a warning to a child regarding their behavior, then follow through.

When you start thinking this way, two things will happen inside of you. First, you will slow down the frequency of threats that you make because you know that you need to follow through. Also, you will evaluate the intensity of threats.

One thing about threats: they don't work.

THREATS DON'T WORK

Why don't threats work? Think about it this way. Your boss keeps coming in your office for two weeks reminding you of a date that a report is due. She says, "If it's not on my desk on November 12th, then I'm writing you up." November 12 comes and goes, you had some crazy things happen in your family and you just couldn't get it done.

Then in January she does the same thing for the report due January 29th. Again you miss the mark and it comes and goes, yet no write up. Imagine this happened over 18 years in the company. Sometimes she does write you up sometimes she doesn't.

Now imagine a different scenario. At a staff meeting she announces that reports need to be timely. To try

Control vs. Voice

and help the staff keep it in their mind, if the November 12th report is in on time you will get an overnight at the hotel of your choice and if not, then you will be written up.

No more reminders.

Then she does what she says.

Often parents believe that they have a voice in their child's life and that is enough, but really a voice is earned through consistency. Your action of giving positive or negative consequences will speak more than anything you could say ahead of time or threaten.

Even when threats do seem to work, it is usually not based on building a long-term voice in your child's life.

The second part of this is building love. I trust that you love your child deeply; otherwise you would not be reading this book. So it is not how to build your love for your child that is the issue, it is how do children receive love?

Consistency in parenting helps kids feel safe. If you are about to manage a child in a grocery store and help her choose good choices there, then you can definitely take on any monster, bad dream, bully, and tornado. Kids fear all sorts of things.

A psychologist named Maslow created what he called the "Hierarchy of Needs". His belief was that if basic needs are not met is it is harder or impossible to work toward higher needs. Thus, if safety needs of security aren't met, it is harder to build feelings of love and belonging.

I had a client recently who had her apartment broken into. She was staying up all night because she was scared someone would break in, then she was sleeping during the day, but her classes were slipping. Her feelings of lack of safety made it harder for her to do more complex thinking like that which is required in school.

Control vs. Voice

The same is true for kids, as they see that you can handle a variety of situations, they will trust that you can protect them.

SETTING AN EXAMPLE

Not only do kids build trust through feeling safe, but they also begin to trust you through your actions in everyday life.

I was working with a family a while ago and the teenager had anger issues. He would yell, kick holes in the walls, and tip over furniture.

As I talked with the parents, they denied any out of the ordinary anger in their lives. Yet, as I built rapport with them, it came out that the mother had a drinking problem. She would only drink once a month, but when she did she was remarkably mean and angry. She would bring up things from the month that she had been bottling up. This is an extreme example that demonstrates how a child feels they have permission to do what you do in their own way.

Often parents won't realize they are inadvertently giving their children permission to misbehave. A child can take a flippant comment you make driving in a different direction. Kids unknowingly say to themselves, "Mom insulted that bad driver, that kid on the playground is bad at baseball, so I can insult him."

CREATING A SPARK

This year I planted a garden. I knew that I could not top last year's garden. We had a baby in May and I knew that what I planted would not be attended to. Weeds grew as high as the corn. The basil produced, but all the tomato plants died. Two of the lettuce seeds grew. I only got two green peppers. I knew that I was raising something better than a garden, my daughter!

I noticed something interesting in mid-June. There was this random vine growing in the middle of the garden. I supported it with a small tomato cage. In mid-August I noticed blossoms. It was a cherry tomato vine that was from a seed of a tomato from last year! I produced more tomatoes than all the planted vines.

It is similar with kids. You never know what experience, art class, play date, or vacation is going to inspire them. Building trust in your child can occur through offering new experiences. As kids grow, they rarely remember all of the small failed attempts as sparking something in them. Yet what they do remember is the feeling they got when they rode a horse for the first time, their painting was selected for a kid's art show, or the time you climbed that mountain.

Creating a spark in your kids is usually more random than the other things I have discussed. It's behind every corner and invisible. So what is a parent to do?

First, learning with your child is a great way for you both to feel vulnerable and try something new. If you go on a vacation, research things that will stretch everyone's comfort zones.

Second, don't push them too hard. There is something to be said for encouraging your child to keep with piano or stick with soccer. But at some point you have allow your child to say that it's just not for them.

Lastly, always encourage play, even when they are older. There are more research studies than I have time to quote that show that time outside, away from media builds creativity and imagination. Do your best to help them get outside in age-appropriate play.

So as you seek to have a voice in your child's life, rather than control, you will see that it is easier to be consistent, to set an example, and create spark moments.

To summarize:

1. Your goal is not to control your child, but rather to have a voice in their life that they trust.

2. Threats: they don't work. Being consistent over time helps your child know they can trust you.

Control vs. Voice

3. Don't give your child permission to misbehave by not parenting or setting a bad example.

4. Create a spark in your child by investigating what makes them tick. Give them new experiences.

BIG DATES, FIRST DAYS OF SCHOOL, AND TICKETS

Once we clearly identify behavior and meet those basic needs, we can move on to teaching the behavior.

I often get sick of the "Everyone is number one" approach to kids. I understand that for a long time no one knew anything about self esteem. Now a growing number of kids seem to have a sense of entitlement.

This is common in highly developed and affluent cultures. When kids routinely believe that they have achieved something when they have not, there is not a feeling of failure and, thus, some intrinsic motivation to avoid failure is lost.

With that said, appropriately learning to praise children is an art. As is any art, it takes practice, finesse, and a touch of luck. Some are more gifted at it than others.

When praise is used as part of a parenting plan, rather than as a way to boost self-esteem it teaches to children's behavior and gives them feedback on how to adjust it accordingly. As I have worked with over two thousand kids over the past ten years, I have seen this cycle: expectations, behavior, feedback, and consequences. This has changed kid's and parent's lives.

EXPECTATIONS

Expectations are different from threats. Expectations are discussed during a neutral time: before going into the grocery store, before a big date, before driving alone for the first time, or before going to school.

Depending on your child, you can change these words. "Expectations" is a fairly strong word, similar to control, reward or punishment. Words like "wish" or "opinion" may be more comfortable for you; however, they also don't carry the same weight until your kids see positive and negative consequences flow out of that "wish" or "opinion."

Big Dates, First Days of School, and Tickets

An expectation typically carries with it a specific description of behavior. Phrases like "Be good" or "Act your age" don't help shape and change behavior as clearly as a more detailed description like "I want you to say, 'Hello' to the other kids and shake their hands," or "You need to drive only to the destinations we discussed and be home by 10:00" or "When we're in the store, please don't ask for cereal or candy."

By giving an expectation, you're setting an "anchor-point" to return to later. When an inappropriate behavior does occur, you can say, "Remember our conversation in the car about cereal?" "It's 10:15, do you remember our conversation before you left with the car?"

BEHAVIOR

Behaviors are things that we as parents can see. They are not feelings, they are not emotions, they are not thoughts. A tantrum is not a behavior; it is a description that captures a bunch of behaviors. Stomping your feet, rolling your eyes, throwing things, laying on the floor and kicking and screaming and throwing Cheerios over the floor that I just swept and now I have to do it again...those are descriptions of behavior. "Tantrum" is not a description of behavior.

As a parent, you will need to practice describing your child's behavior. Imagine you were watching a video of your child's behavior and you had a friend with you that is blind. How would you describe it?

"Austin is having a tantrum in this video," you might start.
"What do you mean?" your friend might ask.
"He's kicking his feet, laying on the floor, and being defiant."
"What do you mean by defiant?"

You can see how this conversation could go, if they really wanted to learn what Austin is doing you can't use words like "tantrum," "inappropriate," ""defiant," or "bad." These are all words that capture descriptions of behaviors. We sort of know what it means, but it's not as clear as just noting the actual behavior.

So first you'll set the expectations by explaining what you want your child to do. Then you will observe what they end up doing. Next you will give them feedback.

FEEDBACK

Feedback used to be the hardest part of parenting for you, but if you've done a good job in the first two steps, than you've already laid the ground work. Your expectation, if clear enough, should have left no questions about what you wanted. By watching what your child does, they should know if they have done it as well as you. Thus, the feedback should be the easiest part.

Let me pause right here.

It is not going to be easy at first. In fact, it is going to be terrible, it will probably suck, and be a personal sort of hell that makes you question why you even thought to disrupt the apple cart of your parenting. Here is a quick story that I tell parents in my practice.

Mental Wellness Parenting

When I was in my Bachelors studies, I had to take a PSY 360 class. The class itself was mostly memorization, but the rat lab was where I learned the most about psychology, behavior, and behavior change.

I had trained a rat to push a lever five times, pull a string, push a marble, pull the string again, which then turned on a light. The rat had learned that when the light came on if he pushed the lever ten times he would get a drink of water. This took about six weeks of training four hours per week. Then we had to extinguish the behavior. My role was to never turn on the light and count how many times the rat pushed the lever.

I have never seen anything like it.

That rat pushed the lever over 200 times. In the past, he pushed it a total of 15 times and got what he wanted. He tried pushing the marble, pulling the string, but nothing worked. He panicked, had a rat tantrum, and went back to pushing the level. Now what do you think would have happened if I had turned on the light after 200 times? How many times would he push it the next time? 400? 500?

What if I turned on the light after 500 pushes?

Might this rat's behavior escalate? Would it become inappropriate? Extreme?
The same is true with your child. As you develop new approaches, they are not going to believe that you have changed in this way; they will try the old way of pushing the marble and pulling the string and pushing the level, instead of 15 times, 200 times. They will push back.

But what happened with the rat? I never turned on the light. In the next session, he only pushed it 100 times. The next session it was 50 times. The next session he tried 10 times and gave up. Rather than keep escalating his behavior to get what he wanted, he realized that the old approach was no longer useful. What is important with kids is to understand this rewiring of the brain. It is like two roads.

CONSEQUENCES

The wires in your child's brain are like two roads. One is a well-developed highway with three lanes, exit ramps, and rest areas. The other is barely a trail. The way that you have done parenting has laid the wonderful and smooth road. Your new approaches to parenting are the trail.

Each time that you build trust through consistency, setting an example, and sparking something in them, you are walking down the new trail. Over time, that new trail becomes wider, trees get cut down and eventually you can drive a car down that two track.

At the same time, the things you don't like about your old way need to slowly deteriorate. That old highway needs to develop some potholes, the grass needs to start growing through the cracks, and trees need to remain un-pruned around the edges.

Then there is a point where the new road is maybe a dirt road and the old road is really bumpy and overgrown. Maybe the new road has been going well for a while, but your child realizes that neither road is established in her brain. This is the second major dip. After months of improving, their old behaviors jump back up and they give it one last ditch effort. You as a parent can nurture the new road or go back to the old one.

Now what happens is parents sometimes cave at this point because they think the new way is not working. In reality, just the opposite is occurring. The new way of parenting is actually gaining some strength and your child wants to know if they can trust that this will "stick." Should I follow what mom is saying or is this just a phase?

I had a family in practice that let the child know their expectation, watched his behavior, and then gave feedback. But they weren't seeing dramatic changes. It was because they were missing the final step of consequences. As a general rule of thumb, you want to be giving feedback on positive behavior about five times more than giving feedback on negative behavior.

John Gottman, a leading marriage researcher, notes this in marriages as well. The five times rule tends to be something valuable in all human relationships, not just as a parent.

Usually the giving of a positive or negative consequence speaks volumes more than any feedback you give. But the feedback, if clear, will help your child quickly adjust their behavior when they see it tied to a consequence.
Here are some quick definitions:

Positive Consequence: Anything that increases a behavior (a high five, ice cream, additional privileges, time with friends).
Negative Consequence: Anything that decreases the frequency of a behavior (chores, loss of privileges, time outs).

I was working with a mom a few years ago. Initially she came to see me because her ten year old son had major anger issues. For example, when he was told "no" he tipped over furniture, tried to hit his mother, and refused to do just about anything. Initially he was coming to therapy and she was supportive. After six months of very little progress, the mother asked what more we could do.

We decided to shift to focusing on a family-wide plan, not just one for the ten-year-old son. She began coming to therapy without her son. We started with a house contract to set expectations it looked something like this:

Sanok Family Contract

For each of the following you may earn a ticket each day:

1. Getting your homework done before dinner is served at 5:30.
2. If you do not physically hurt a member of the house or hurt family property during the entire day.

3. You complete one chore. You have to ask mom what chore she would like for you to do.

These tickets will be able to be redeemed when the "Mom Store" is open Tuesdays at 4:00 or additional times determined by Mom.

Also, for each ticket earned, there will be a chart; whoever earns 50 tickets first may get take-out from the restaurant of their choice or whoever has the most at the end of the month.

Signed,

Mom

Remember the concept of working toward something positive vs. avoiding something negative? This is exactly how it could look for you!

Big Dates, First Days of School, and Tickets

The "Mom Store" had everything from 5 ticket cheap items to higher priced 20 oz. Mt. Dews, video games, coloring books, and other items the kids wanted. Similar to those rip off games at bowling alleys, each item had a ticket amount. All the items were on display in a locked cabinet to tempt them daily. Mom set the expectation, and then watched the behavior. The tendency of most parents is to then remind the kids. But what this mom did is when her son asked for a soda she would reply, "You'll have to buy it with your tickets on Tuesday."

"Mom I want chips."
"You'll have to earn tickets by Tuesday then."
"Can't I just pay you back later?"
"Nope, you'll need to plan ahead."

So in addition to building expectations, she was also building the social skill of planning ahead. What happened is that at first all the kids tried hard for two days. Then the original ten-year-old kid gave up. He didn't believe that the system was going to stick. He tried getting his mom to cave in by his old behaviors.

So while his siblings earned chips, soda, and video games, he did not.

It is important to note that you also have to know your child. What is progress for him or her? For the ten-year-old, his attempts at progress may be different from his higher functioning brothers and sister. Eventually he began to comply. As well, the competitive nature of the month-long competition built off of his desire to "beat" his brothers in something.

Lastly, this program would not have worked if he could get the sodas, video games, and chips from another source. If he had an allowance that was not based on positive behavior and they lived next to a 7-11, why would he do his homework, a chore, and act good, then wait until next Tuesday, when he could just go next door?

Big Dates, First Days of School, and Tickets

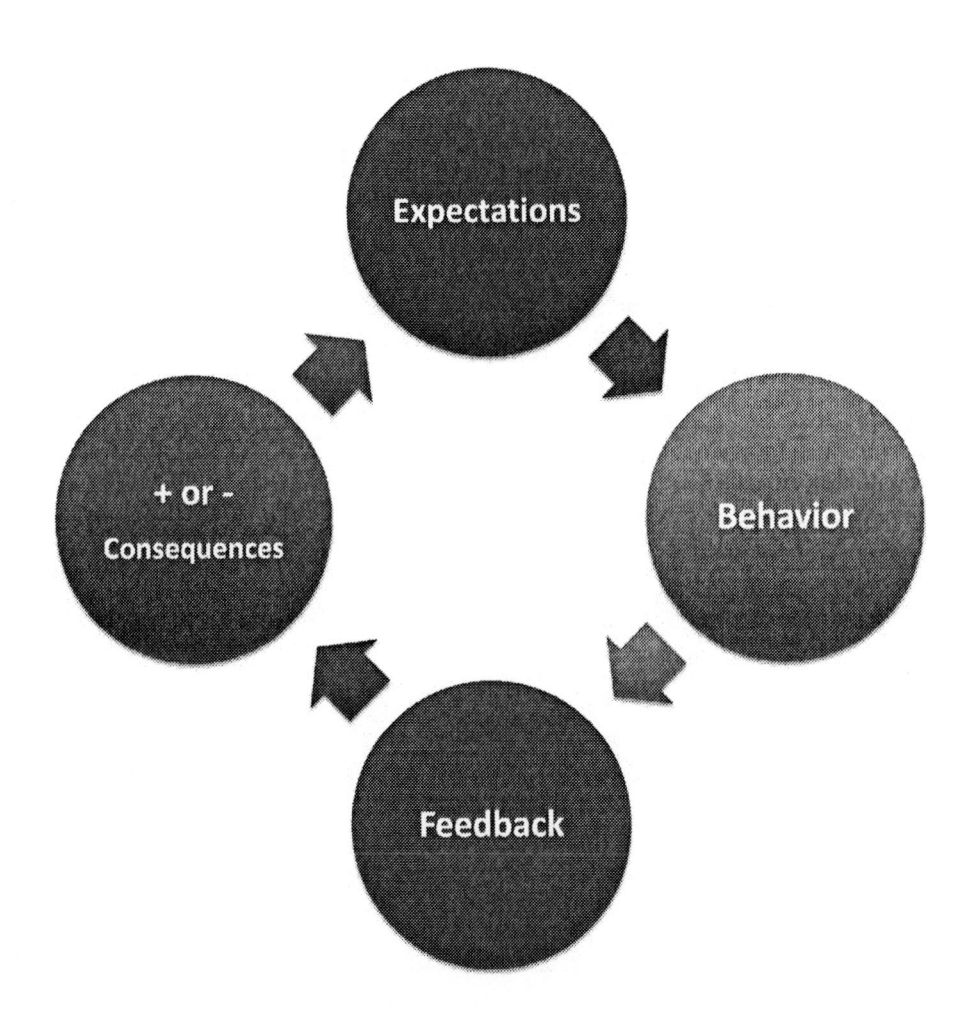

```
        Expectations
       ↙           ↘
+ or -              Behavior
Consequences
       ↖           ↙
         Feedback
```

Like water, kids will take the easiest route. Therefore, if you want to change behavior, make your route the only way they can get there. When kids know what to expect and are able to better predict what the outcome will be, they have less anxiety and thus, less behavior that is not appropriate. Further, when they feel they can change outcomes, they feel empowered and have a boost in their self-esteem.

I think about my own journey. When I was in second grade I wanted a skateboard. My parents gave me a clear way to acquire the skateboard. I had to ear half of the money, which at the time was $20. To a child with no job and no means, this would have been an impossible task. But then they said, "The neighbors are going on vacation; I bet they need someone to put water in their birdbath each day. Maybe you should go ask them."

I imagine that my parents called them and maybe even gave them the $20 for me filling the birdbath for five days. But the point of the exercise was that I had to muster enough courage to speak to semi-strangers, follow-through with my job, and report to them when they returned home. That skateboard meant so much to me.

When I was in the Boy Scouts we had to earn money to go on a trip scuba diving in Florida. My parents let

Big Dates, First Days of School, and Tickets

me know that I would have to pay all of the $700. For me, it caused mild anxiety as a teen, but it did not seem impossible. I had built those skills over the year.

In high school, I decided that I wanted to go to Europe after my freshman year of college. I saved all of my graduation money and put it into a 6-month certificate of deposit to come due around the time I would have to buy plane tickets for my six week adventure.

Throughout all of this, I had learned skills that built upon one another. The path my parents gave me was the easiest to achieve my goals. They walked with me, but ultimately I had to take those final steps. I had less anxiety each time because I had a framework to draw from. At times we overestimate our kid's abilities and set them free without giving them appropriate skills. At other times, we don't let them take enough steps on their own.

May you have wisdom to know the difference between the two.

To summarize:

1. Expectations are discussed during a neutral time and are an anchor point for future discussions.

2. Feedback comes in two forms: positive and negative consequences. Positive consequences increase the likelihood of the behavior occurring. Negative consequences decrease the likelihood of the behavior occurring.

3. Kids will work toward something positive more often than avoid something negative.

4. Skills build upon one another over the lifetime of a person.

PURPOSE?

Recently my daughter has been going through a growth spurt. She's a few months old; she's breastfeeding, and starting to smile a lot more, especially when I get home from work. The other night, we realized that our daughter would take a bottle better than the breast. In fact, she drank seven ounces, rather than her usual one or two.

The only way that we could get her to drink from mom was to start with a pacifier, and then trick her into drinking breast milk from mom, but even then it was only temporary.

Then it hit my wife that maybe she'd never want to drink from her again.
Isn't this how parenting goes?

It's pretty much a series of events where your child moves away from you. First they are inside you, or in my case, inside my wife. They are dependent on you even to hold up their head. They then lift their head, wiggle their legs, roll over, crawl, walk, run, say "no," go to pre-school, still snuggle with you, then somewhere they stop snuggling, they want to spend the night at a friend's house, they go to birthday parties without you, they want you to drop them off a block away from school, they start driving, go to college, get married...parenting is a list of things kids do to move away from us.

At the heart of being a parent is this dichotomy between grief and joy. We love to see our kids in their success, but we also long for the stages that are now gone. Maybe another way of saying this is that:

Our role as a parent is to help our kids successfully go.

When you think about any parenting advice, the end result is the same. If someone says that we should raise kids to be good citizens, how does that happen? Only if they are competent adults can they do this. Some say, we should raise kids to honor God, for them

Purpose?

to be good parents, for them to be ecological, for them to be (fill in the blank), this doesn't happen unless they have appropriately left us.

They key here is "appropriately." Many kids leave their parents. The goal is not go them to never talk to us, consult with us, or ask our advice. But, our role shifts over time from parent to guide, mentor, and consultant.

The framework is the same no matter the age of your child: review behavior, encourage more autonomy, and give feedback.

REVIEW BEHAVIOR

You know your child best. When you build your parenting approach, knowing what is "normal" for your child is important. You have learned that behaviors are things that we as parents can see. They are not feelings, they are not emotions, they are not thoughts. You can read parenting books, look at things online, and talk to friends, but ultimately you have to know what your child's normal is.

When you have a baseline, I like to think about this as their Comfort Area, these are things that they do naturally. The next area is their Growth Area. These are things that are good for them, expand their horizons, and help them see the world through a new lens. Lastly is their Panic Area. This is when they shut down, freak out, and give up. For some kids, spending the night at another kid's house is Panic Area material, whereas having a child spend the night at your house may be Growth Area. For other kids, it's all Comfort Area.

For your teen asking a friend for homework might be Growth Area. Asking a girl out on a date might be Growth Area or maybe Panic. You want to be aware enough of your child's habits to know their "Growth Area", so that you can help them be successful in that, without them shutting down and panicking.

ENCOURAGE MORE AUTONOMY

Kids usually can handle more than we think. In the book, *Last Child in the Woods,* Richard Louv discusses

Purpose?

a playground in a city where there are piles of boards, tires, and other unused construction materials.

Before kids can play, create, and build, they have to go through a safety course on how to use tools like hand saws and hammers and how to be observant of overall safety. Parents sign a waiver. Then the kids are free to construct forts, obstacle courses, and whatever else they can think of.
The playground is always changing, growing, and being torn apart and rebuilt. Little kids running, playing, and hammering tires upside down to a balance beam they just hammered.

When encouraging more autonomy and independence, most parents worry. A common concern that I hear is that a child will get abducted or get involved with a stranger. Later in the book I discuss the myth of "Stranger Danger" in depth. The quick answer I have is that you should be more concerned about your child being injured in the car you drive. But we'll talk more about strangers later.

Questions you should ask as you and your child build their autonomy:

What are your child's next steps towards autonomy?

How are your issues getting in the way of this growth?

What are you most scared of in your child's behavior?

What is growth for your child?

GIVE FEEDBACK

The last step is to give your child feedback. In previous chapters you learned that this step becomes easier when you have done a good job in the prior steps. In teaching a new or difficult behavior, your expectation, should have left no questions about what you wanted. But, in this situation, you are offering less critique and more noticing.

Purpose?

That is where a few other life and parenting concepts come in to help us in this journey.

CONSEQUENCES

If I fly down Front St. going 55 mph, I will get a ticket. Maybe not the first time, maybe not the second, but it will come. If I stop showing up for work, I will not get paid. If I am not nice to my friends or my wife, eventually they will not want to be with me. Consequences are a part of adult life.

We are preparing our children for the real world through the world we create in our home. Some parents have told me, "I'm just not into punishing my kids." Or, "I want them to be creative and explore the world."

You can both prepare your kids through boundaries and consequences while also allowing them to be magnificently unique individuals. When children experience boundaries and consequences, they feel safer and know what to expect. As well, they can adjust their behavior to meet your expectations.

The quickest step you can take is to clarify what you want. Instead of telling your child, "You're acting inappropriate" or "act your age" say specifically what they should change: rolling their eyes, stomping their feet, not starting their homework when asked. Think of yourself as a narrator instructing them with what you specifically want them to do.

Once you establish a clear expectation, go back to it. "Remember earlier when I asked you to start your homework? You are not doing what I asked." Make it simple and don't expect them to change right away. Kid's brains have been wired from experiences and it takes time to undo the old expectations and start following the new ones.

It's like building a new road in their brains. The old one needs to stop getting usage and the new road needs to grow from a two-track, to a road, to a highway. As you are consistent, it keeps connecting neuropathways to build the new road, while the old one falls apart.

Purpose?

The two strongest negative consequences are a loss of a privilege or giving a chore. What I like about these two negative consequences is that they are time-limited. Rather than ground a child for days, try something like, "Because you did not do your homework when you were asked, you will need to sweep the kitchen after dinner. When you are done sweeping you can go back to watching TV or doing something you like."

Lastly, giving positive consequences can be the most effective strategy. Most research says that kids need to hear what they are doing correctly five times more often than what they are not doing correct.

As you describe behavior, return to those expectations, and give both positive and negative consequences you're preparing them for a successful adulthood.

To summarize:

1. **Parenthood is a series of painful moments when your child is moving away from you.**
2. **Create a baseline for your child's behavior and review the behavior with them as a participant, not just as an observed.**
3. **Push your child toward more autonomy and allow them to experience natural consequences while also teaching them skills to succeed.**
4. **As kids learn new behaviors, their brains are creating new roads. As those new roads are built, kids can react in a variety of ways until the new "road" is established.**

LIFE TIPS THAT APPLY TO PARENTING

The following tips are from a few places I have been published. I hesitated to share them with you, but the audience response has been so overwhelming I thought I'd pass some of them along. Also, there is a whole community of parents, professionals, and learners that are engaging deeper through the Mental Wellness Parenting Facebook Page, will you JOIN THE DISCUSSION?

SLOWING DOWN

I can't slow down. I need this chapter more than anyone. I have a baby, house, job, private practice...the list goes on and on. I bet your list is similar. There is always a reason why I can't slow down.

I went to Michigan's Upper Peninsula this past weekend. It is a quiet part of Michigan where the pace is slower and trees out number people by about a thousand to one.

I sat and drank coffee, looked out at the morning water, and read a magazine. Why is it that when we get away from town, we let ourselves relax? These are three things that are starting to work for me (I'm not there yet).

PUT IT IN THE SCHEDULE

Did you know that 15 minutes is 1% of your day? I think we actually have time to relax for 15 minutes; we just don't make the time. If something is written down, we're more likely to follow through. Plan to relax. When we schedule time and make it a habit, it helps our kids to learn from us, while also teaching us to slow down.

GET OUT

When we are in our houses, we see the laundry, cleaning, and opportunities to not relax. Planning time out of our house clears our mind and gives us permission to forget about the struggles for a space of time. Get away from your house. In doing so, we often have ideas that apply to both parenting and just living life outside of that role.

DRAG IT OUT

When I do errands, I fight for the closest parking spot, hurry in, hurry out, and run back home. There have been times when we have gone to the Farmer's Market and parked a few blocks away. We strolled, looked at the river, and we didn't hurry home. Drag out the time that you are out and about.

But why should we slow down? Shouldn't we be more efficient and productive? Yes, this is true. There are times during the week that productivity and efficiency are of value. Yet, if we make it a lifestyle, we increase our stress, which can lead to a lower quality of sleep, which increases anxiety and depression, while lowering our quality of life.

When you step back, why are you in such a hurry and what is it doing to you? Try it for a day and see if it makes you feel better.

MARRIAGE ISSUES AND MONEY

Over and over, I hear that money is the primary reason for divorce. That is wrong.

Money is not the issue. Money is a tangible example of what a person values and in turn what a couple values. When it is viewed through that lens, it takes some of the emotional explosiveness out of the equation. The real discussion is not about money, but about goals and values.

DETERMINE WHAT YOU WANT

When I work with couples, we don't talk about money, we talk about goals. As a couple, try sitting down, across from one another, without distractions. What are your one-year and five-year goals? Is it to have enough money for a vacation each year so that you can connect more with your family? Is it to not have the stress of a credit card? Is it to have an emergency fund so that you feel more secure?

Do you see how each of those questions is not about the money, but instead about the emotion behind the money?

NAGGING DOES NOT STOP SPENDING

Once you have come together and identified a longer term goal and the emotions behind it, it is easier for couples to make new decisions with their money. Say you decide to save $1,000 for an emergency fund, then that delicious $5 latte seems a little less appealing. What happens is you start to realize that you're choosing an immediate pleasure (a fancy coffee), for a feeling of insecurity (not having an emergency fund).

REWARD YOURSELF

When my wife and I were paying off debt, we'd reward ourselves when we paid something off. For example, if we were paying $250 extra on our car, the month after we paid off the car we spent $250 on us. It was fun, motivating, and it brought us together as a couple.

When couples view money, paying off debt, and saving as an effort that you both are working on, it can bring you together. Remember, budgets and planning how you spend your money are not chains to enslave you, rather, you are telling your money where to go. It is freeing and if done correctly, will bring you together as a couple.

Marriage is really hard work. Weddings tap into the optimism of love and the Hollywood ending. We join couples in their joy and are often inspired when we leave a wedding.

Often as the summer wedding blitz closes and the autumn of marriage is beginning we lose what we may have gained in those experiences.

PROTECT YOUR TIME

Marriage researcher, John Gottman, talks about a couple's tendency to drift away from one another. In his book, *Seven Principles for Making Marriage Work*, he uses the term "parallel lives". It is easy for a couple to drift into being more like roommates than life partners. When you protect your time from over-commitment and things-that-seem-necessary-but-really-aren't you can focus on things that invigorate you as a couple.

CARE DEEPLY ABOUT SOMETHING TOGETHER

Have you ever volunteered with someone? It is amazing how a kinship develops when you help make the world better. It is easy for couples to care deeply about kids and family and soccer games. Volunteering together outside of your house is a sure-fire way to build intimacy and connection as a couple.

BUILD OPEN AND HONEST COMMUNICATION

Even as I write this, I think, "duh." Yet, small secrets and not knowing about the nuances of one another's lives can pull couples apart. Also, minor dishonesty will slowly build into more. In past articles I have discussed boundaries with opposite-sex friends and how those boundaries improve depth in the relationship. Each day we have the opportunity to be more open and honest with our partner to strengthen the relationship.

As you protect your time, care deeply about something, and build better communication, you will see that you improve the dynamic of your marriage away from parallel lives and a little closer to the excitement of your wedding day.

Life Tips That Apply to Parenting

FRIENDS AND CRISIS: DOS AND DON'TS

You never really appreciate a life of normality until crisis hits. Our family has been through a number of things lately a death, a major medical issue, and close friends having their own crisis. It is amazing how it seems that high profile events bring out people's true social skills.

I learned through experience what not to say when someone is in crisis. It was several years ago. I heard that friend of mine's parents had got divorced. I was close to my friend, but not to his parents. During a large festival in our town, I ran into the mom and said, "I'm so sorry to hear about you and _____." It seemed to be the right thing to say. She broke down crying in the middle of the festival.

I felt terrible, I didn't know how to leave, and I regretted saying anything. After that I was fairly gun-shy. When I heard that people had a miscarriage, death, or sickness, I didn't know what to say. So I just watched from a distance. Now that I am going through my own experiences, I feel that I have an understanding of what has worked and not worked for me.

FOOD

<u>Do</u>

Make or bring food. It allows the family to focus on one another, rather than shopping, cooking, and cleaning.

Try and make something they can freeze or bring it frozen so that if others are bringing food they can pull it out when it works.

If you can, use things you don't need back like Tupperware, something disposable, or a pan you don't care about. Tell them, "Don't worry about getting the pan back to me."

<u>Don't</u>

Don't expect to hang out with the family long.

Life Tips That Apply to Parenting

Don't just show up, call and ask if there is a convenient time.

TALKING

Do

Empathize with the family. Our friends that have said, "That must be hell" "I can't imagine going through that" and "When will the universe stop shi**ing on the Sanok's?" have been some of the most helpful comments. It makes us not feel crazy.

Let the family or person do the talking. Saying, "If you don't feel like talking about it, that's ok, but how are you doing?" is helpful because it is nice to be given permission to blow someone off and stay quiet.

Don't

Don't offer suggestions unless you are asked. If people are dealing with medical issues, they probably are consulting with the doctors. If they are going through a death, their closest friends will probably know what/when to suggest therapy. In general, suggestions make people feel like you want to solve their problems and make them move through their grief, rather than be with them.

EXPECTATIONS

Do

Expect that your relationship will be different for a while. They may see you more or less. They may want to sit at home and drink. They may not want to talk. Realize that people handle crisis very differently and the way they react can differ too.

Don't

Don't get offended when they focus on something other than your relationship. If you do get offended, don't show it. Months later if it is still bothering you, you can talk with that person.

Life Tips That Apply to Parenting

Don't worry about spending too much or too little time with them. Ask them if it would be helpful to come over.

Don't say, "Call us if you need anything." Say something more specific like, "Would it be helpful if we had you over for dinner? We'd love to have you, but you can totally say 'no'." Sometimes what people need is awkward to ask for like a gas card. Rather than ask, "What do you need?" say something like, "Here's a gas card/meal/hug if it would help." By giving the person an out and being specific, it helps to give them the power and control, when life seems out of control.

Depending on which side of the crisis you are (going through it or supporting through it) everyone should realize that you are lucky to have one another. As someone going through life issues, I am so thankful for people saying and doing something, even if they fumble through it. Despite the missteps some have taken, we have realized that it is all done out of love and care for us.

I would much rather have someone awkwardly try and console me, than to remain quiet out of fear…and then go through a crisis alone.

Do you want a copy of my, "Guide for Times Like These" handout on this topic? Go to: http://www.mentalwellnesscounseling.com/tragedy/

BLAH IN OUR BRAINS

I hate when there is the winter time change. I don't understand why during the darkest part of the year, we make it darker. I would much rather have it stay dark until 10:00 am and have light in the evening. But maybe that's just me.

During fall and winter lack of light triggers in people a sense of fatigue, sadness, depression, and feelings of blah. Whether you deal with clinical depression, seasonal affective disorder, or feelings of blah, there are several things you can do that will help you feel better.

Life Tips That Apply to Parenting

GET MORE LIGHT

Even when it is light outside, it seems to still be cloudy in Northern Michigan. A window usually is not enough. Regular lights do not capture the full light spectrum. They usually only have the blues and violets. Getting outside and sitting by a window will help, but changing some of your bulbs in your office or home to full-spectrum light bulbs can really help. A number of studies have shown that full-spectrum light can help with depression, sadness, and the feelings of blah (blah is not a clinical term used in research studies). Bulbs usually run $14-$24 dollars, a lot cheaper than therapy.

GET MORE EXERCISE

Exercise releases natural endorphins in your body. I was at the University of Michigan Depression Conference last year and one speaker was discussing how some studies are showing that exercise paired with counseling can be more effective than psychiatric medication. Even a short walk or taking the stairs can be helpful.

GET MORE VEGGIES

Fruits and vegetables can help with replenishing the body's nutrients. Loads of colors in your diet are helpful. A diet of reduced processed foods helps to make the brain more receptive to light and exercise during the winter months. WedMD has a number of helpful nutrition suggestions, http://www.webmd.com/depression/guide/diet-recovery

GET MORE SOCIALIZATION

When I work with clients dealing with depression they often get into a cycle of alone time. They don't feel like going out or doing anything which makes them feel like they don't want to go out and do anything. During winter months we often feel like we want to hunker down and stay home. Socialization and new activities help us free up the blah in our brain.

Life Tips That Apply to Parenting

Once you try these tips, you will hopefully see changes. With that said, you also need to know when to talk with your health care provider about pursuing additional options.

As with any change, it is better to start small and make little changes that you can do. Maybe for you a step would be to change a light bulb, go for a daily walk, eat broccoli again, or plan a potluck with friends or family. The hardest part is taking a step in the right direction, after that you will pick up momentum and have a blah-free winter.

OPTIMIST'S CREED

Often as I am falling asleep, my mind takes off. It is like it has somehow been waiting all day until I hit the pillow, then it decides to fire on all cylinders. I toss and turn. I think about the idea or situation from many angles. Sometimes, I remember something I need to do in the morning, like bring something for a work potluck. I hold onto the task and it prevents me from sleeping. Yet, when I write the idea or list item down, it frees my brain. I then know that I will not forget, because it is written down. I am free.

How often do we do this with other things?

The seventh promise of the Optimist's Creed is, "To forget the mistakes of the past and press on to the greater achievements of the future." It sounds so good it should be on a bumper sticker. I am sure it is, but it might be simplified to, "Forget and move on" because if it were longer people would probably run into one another.

When we hear something like this, our pessimistic side often argues about how we've learned from mistakes. We're better people from them. If we let go, we'll also let go of all we've learned. But really, we're just tossing and turning through life.

When we hold onto our mistakes and those that others have done that hurt us, it is like trying to sleep while keeping a mental "to do" list. It is near impossible to fall asleep while holding on to a mental challenge.

So what are we to do?

EXAMINE THE "MISTAKE"

Take some time in a comfortable place, preferably outside of your home. Go somewhere that you can hash through your own mistakes. Take a journal. As you make a list of the mistakes that you or others have committed, list those on a page, or two, or twenty. Go into as much detail as you need. Be your own therapist.

WHAT HAVE YOU LEARNED POSITIVE AND NEGATIVE?

Next, dive into the list and examine what you have learned about the world. At this point, don't judge what you are writing. Instead, just brainstorm. If someone sexually abused you, what did that teach you about the world? When he treated you like crap, what assumptions did you draw? When she said that irreversible statement, what did you say to yourself?

What you learned usually falls into two categories, assumptions about the way the world works and decisions about how you will react to that assumption.

QUESTION THE ACCURACY OF YOUR ASSUMPTIONS

The next step is to assume the role of a skeptic. When we have things occur, especially at a young age, we usually continue those assumptions unless they are challenged by something greater and more powerful later in life. Remember, what happened to you when you were eight was processed by an eight-year-old. The same is true with every other time in your life. You are now more mature and understand other aspects of the world. Use that new knowledge to hash through the former assumptions you created. Those assumptions had a function, but often they no longer help.

LET GO OF THE GUILT AND HOLD ON TO THE TRUE LESSONS

The true lessons in any mistake are often the hardest to discover, because they can be covered with false assumptions and reactions. Often friends, a therapist, or counselor can help challenge these points of view.

One example for me: When I was in eighth grade this classmate just came up to me and started punching me. It was in front of most of my class. I had done nothing. I didn't fight back.

For years, I wished I had fought back. I re-imagined the situation, with me punching, kicking, and showing him what I was made of. I also called myself a wimp, a push over, and someone that was not worth as much as him.

When I look at the situation, his mother was a single mom and he didn't have much money. Our school was fairly affluent. He was always getting into trouble. As a 13 year-old kid, I didn't understand how his poverty, lack of family support, and aggressive behavior all had nothing to do with me. He was probably hurting. Further, that situation put a spotlight on my gentle spirit.

By revisiting these old "mistakes" I see that a counselor spirit was already being formed. I now can let go of my own mistakes and those of others.

May you evaluate, digest, and let go of your past mistakes and those that others have inflicted on you, so that you may be the best future you possible. May you let go so that you can be well rested and present to the world that needs you.

Life Tips That Apply to Parenting

SUICIDE PREVENTION

In 9th grade, the school counselor brought me and several other students into her office. She informed us that a peer had committed suicide. Later, the entire school was informed. It is devastating to get that type of news. Every 15 minutes another family, friend, and school deal with news of a suicide.

Often people think that the issue of suicide prevention is only for mental health professionals, but sometime in each of our lives we will probably have it touch us. Here are a few things that every person should know to help a friend, family member, or co-worker.

IF YOU ARE CONCERNED, ASK

Asking a person if they are suicidal is the best first step. When a person is dealing with intense emotions, friends often feel uncomfortable asking about suicide. However, a direct question from a friend or family member is shown to reduce the risk of suicide.

UNDERSTAND MORE ABOUT SUICIDE

For a number of years, San Francisco has employed interviewers to speak with people who have jumped from the Bay Bridge and survived. One thing that an overwhelming majority report is that during their fall, they regretted the decision and hoped to live. These individuals often became advocates for suicide prevention. Further, research continues to support that suicidal feelings often last only hours, but return if help is not sought.

KNOW RESOURCES

Knowing that you can ask about suicide and that it is often a short-term feeling, getting a friend help is a great first step. Also, supporting the individual through counseling and being a friend is the best role that you can have.

When we as a community work together to help those that are struggling, when we ask, understand, and

Life Tips That Apply to Parenting

refer, it can help reduce suicide. Each one of us can use our relationships and unique roles to be a part of a more healthy community.

QUICK TOPIC LISTS

This final section is meant to help you in a variety of areas.

SIGNS OF STRESS WITH KIDS

1. **Collect data**

    Let's say a mom realizes that her four-year-old daughter Lydia has been acting differently, what might be some signs that Lydia's stress or anxiety isn't normal?

    How do emotions of the parents play into a child's anxiety and stress?

    Often parents react to their children's emotions or their own. As a result, their decisions aren't based on what is really going on; rather, what they feel is going on. Data helps to see patterns of stress related to what is going on in the family and child's life. For example, could the recent anxiety be based on a conversation that Lydia overheard or an event in the family that she does not know how to process?

2. Talk more often

Sometimes it is hard to get younger kids to talk about stress, how do you get them to talk? Asking an open ended question to Lydia like "If you had a million dollars, what would you do with it?" "If you could relive 30 minutes from today, what would you re-live?" will create on-going dialog throughout their life.

3. Look for patterns and themes

Lydia is trying to make sense of the world as a four-year-old. She will look at a variety of media to identify characters she can learn from. Lydia's parent could use media to ask questions like "Which characters do you identify with, Lydia?" (Is Lydia always drawn to the sad character, the hyper one, the leader?)

4. Make changes

Quick Topic Lists

So maybe mom realizes that Lydia may have some stress or anxiety, what can she do? Increase a feeling of safety, reducing TV, increasing sleep, increasing time in nature, and having creative unplanned time are all ways to help kids reduce anxiety and stress.

5. Know when to get extra help

So let's say a mom has been doing all these things and little four-year-old and Lydia doesn't seem to be responding at preschool, but she's doing better at home, what should they do then? When do you try to improve their environment vs. say going to counseling? Should you talk to other people in little Lydia's life?

When a child seems to be having trouble across multiple environments, despite the interventions, this is a key time to speak with a professional. Or, if there are environments where she is doing better, it can be helpful to identify variables that are helping that can be applied to other situations.

As you evaluate your youth's data, youth time talking with him/her, have looked for patterns talk, and patterns, there is a point where you know that something is not going right. Talk to their teacher, care givers, bus driver, friend's parents. If it is environment-specific it can be a behavioral reaction, whereas if it is across environments it may be a growing psychological disorder.

HOW TO BE A PARENT, NOT A FRIEND

1. Say "no" more

    Boundaries are important

    Kids want to know that you are in control

2. Prevent bad behavior

    Teach expectations

    Break down social skills into easy steps

3. Vent to your friends, not your kids

    It promotes your healthiness

    Mommy/Daddy time teaches your kids when to be with you and when to find their own things to do.

Quick Topic Lists

4. Don't seek to make them happy, be happy with what they seek

    Your goal as a parent is to teach them how to be adults, to transition into what they can be. Encourage dreams, not short term goals that they want now.

Go to http://www.mentalwellnesscounseling.com/2013-goals/ for my "Setting Goals" handout

IF YOU DON'T DO THIS, YOUR SCHOOL YEAR WILL SUCK

Here are some quick bullet points to help with school-year routines. Of course each one could be expanded further, but hopefully by now you have learned the basic concepts of *Mental Wellness Parenting* so you can expand them yourself.

Bedtime

Determine weekend bedtime on how well they go to bed during the week. Friends over or fun activities should be based on if the child did homework or worked on an area of concern (such as reading).

Set a schedule that includes a clear bedtime

Scheduling

The daily schedule should be the same during the week. With busy schedules try and have homework be right when they get home, snack, relax/activity, dinner, bed prep.

1. Wake up with plenty of time
2. Have breakfast
3. Have them do their morning and evening routine in the same order each night so they know what to expect.

Quick Topic Lists

Talking to you kid's teacher

1. Find out last year's concerns and discuss options for the coming year
2. What is their teaching style and what goals do they have for them (reading/math benchmarks)

Media and screen time

During the week try and turn off the TV as much as possible. You can TiVo/DVR/Hulu for the weekend. According to the A.C. Nielsen Co: Number of minutes per week that parents spend in meaningful conversation with their children: 3.5. Compare that to the number of minutes per week that the average child watches television: 1,680 (28 hours a week, 4 a day).

Sleep

Teach your child how to sleep and eat well by:

1. Have a routine: fan, tucking them in, checking the locked doors
2. Deep breathing and progressive muscle relaxation
3. TV off at least 30 minutes before bedtime

TEEN DATING

What to do with your dating teen? Four things to think about.

1. **Teen dating issues start way before they're teens.**

    How have you taught them to self-regulate prior to this? Our culture pushes a quick answer approach, Just say "no," but that does not prepare them for the emotions of dating and being pleasure seekers. Throughout their life, parents need to teach kids how to delay pleasure for something bigger. Think about what you're teaching them: healthy male-female relationships vs. just say "no." How would that work in a marriage?

Quick Topic Lists

2. **Make your home conducive to having kids over.**

    If your teens feel a healthy sense freedom at your house and have a place to go (the basement with the ping-pong table where the TV is with a DVD player) they will be more likely to have friends over.

    Make teenager snacks, remember, most kids don't have much money so going to the movies and buying pop and popcorn is not something they can afford to do, food and entertainment is the key to creating a safe and fun place.

3. **Know your teen's friends**

    If you know the influences in your teen's life, it will make dating discussions easier.

4. **Set clear boundaries together**

    "If you'd like to extend your curfew I need to know that I can trust you, let's make a list of acceptable and unacceptable things to do while you're out."

Where, Who, What and how can I get a hold of you?

Remember, they're not just arbitrary rules like "You can't date until you're 16" you're slowly moving them towards adulthood.

FAMILIES AND HOLIDAYS

1. **Give yourself permission to be unique:** sometimes we think we have to have the same holiday traditions that our families had, they may not work for you now. What do you need? Know when you need a break, maybe you should just go to your favorite coffee shop for the afternoon.
2. **Talk to your kids about expectations before the event:** on the drive over to Aunt Mackenzie's, talk about your expectations and how to get out of difficult situations.
3. **Involve your kids in the planning:** Whenever you can, help them to engage in planning. As

Quick Topic Lists

they are a part of it, they will also feel like owners and feel responsible for the success of the event.

4. **Talk openly with your family/partner about what you want:** So often each person has their own expectations for what they want to get out of the holidays, but no one else knows, then they wonder why they're disappointed.

5. **Give yourself permission to shut up:** Is your 91 year old aunt really going to change her political views? Is your uncle going to change his tone of voice? Know what to engage in and when to just listen. You don't have to agree, but some battles just aren't worth fighting, because it's not going to change the person's mind.

Go to http://www.mentalwellnesscounseling.com/holidays/ for my "Getting Through the Holidays" handout about this topic.

Mental Wellness Parenting

GENERAL CONCEPTS FOR ALL AGES

1. Consistency in parenting: Keep a journal of major age decisions if you have more than one child: age of ear piercings, when they could date, how they earn allowance, did they have to pay for their own car insurance, age of first sleep over

2. Setting boundaries early is important.

3. Give your child a chance to fail.

4. Build love and connectedness

ELEMENTARY AGE INDEPENDENCE

Main goal- To learn to socialize, use creativity, and make basic decisions of right and wrong.

Activities-

K-1: friends over to play, time away from the family

Quick Topic Lists

with friends

2-4: Overnights and structured social groups (cub scouts, 4-H)

TWEEN INDEPENDENCE

Main goal- To learn the complexities of social interaction, make connections between behavior and consequences, and plan ahead. They are shaping their identity and will try some weird stuff in the process. Girls need help handling the media images of women; boys need help managing the difference between their feelings and what society says if "manly."

Activities-

Although youth are more moody, challenging, and push you away, they need to know that home is a safe place to "launch" from.

Planned time with friends where independence is gained throughout middle school. Just hanging out at the mall should not be an option, but planning to go to the movies and walking around the hour before with a friend is appropriate.

In general, tweens need to feel like they have independence and choice, while also having the parent check in with them in various ways.

TEEN INDEPENDENCE

Main goal- To move toward living on their own with the skills and knowledge it takes, while choosing which peers they will allow to influence them more than their family. To appropriately challenge their assumptions to find their own voice beyond the family of origin. They are shaping their identity and will try some weird stuff in the process if they didn't do it in their tween years.

Activities-

Quick Topic Lists

Activities that are scheduled with their friends, by senior year, their freedom should be moving towards independence. The more of a shock it is, usually the more poor choices they make.

Examples, time down at Cherry Fest where they check in every 2 hours while you are down there, then moving slowly to more independence.

Teen Frontal Lobe: "the teenager's brain may be responding with more of a gut reaction than an executive or more thinking kind of response. And if that's the case, then one of the things that you expect is that you'll have more of an impulsive behavioral response, instead of a necessarily thoughtful or measured kind of response." From PBS interview with Dr. Yurgelun-Todd from McClean Hospital in MA. Her recent work suggests that teens' brains actually work differently than adults' when processing emotional information from external stimuli.

NOW WHAT?

What are you going to do with this information? What are your next steps? I hope that you have taken the time to stop and take notes of ideas and recommendations. When I read something, I try and do something today that will help me start taking actions. Rather than look at hurdles, look at what you can start on. So often we fail before we start. Here are a few thoughts of what might be helpful:

1. **Take action** on something this week. The sooner you master something, the sooner you can start reaping the rewards.
2. **Find another parent** to join you in this journey. We are communal people. Joining with another parent will help you to be inspired and grow. Also, there is a whole community of parents, professionals, and learners that are engaging deeper through the Mental Wellness Parenting Facebook Page, will you JOIN THE DISCUSSION?

3. **Follow my blog or sign up for my e-newsletter at www.MentalWellnessCounseling.com.** As parents and clinicians respond to what we've discussed, I'll be writing tips, thoughts, and ideas to help you grow your parenting skills.

4. **Review the essential reading list.** On my website, I have a growing list of books that I highly recommend. These are authors that I have learned from and find to be much smarter than myself. They take these concepts to an entirely different level of greatness. http://www.mentalwellnesscounseling.com/resources/

Never stop learning; your kids need you more than ever!

Quick Topic Lists

A Quick Note from Joe:

Thank you so much for joining me in this journey. I hope that is was valuable for you. I would love to hear from you, what did you like/hate/use? Also,

If you liked it and want others to read it, please send them to my blog www.MentalWellnessCounseling.com.

Thank you so much!!!
If you have questions, let's talk:

Joe

joe@mentalwellnesscounseling.com

Mental Wellness Parenting

Quick Topic Lists

RESOURCES

COUNSELING SUBJECTS

My blog and social media connections for counseling and family issues: www.mentalwellnesscounseling.com/

www.twitter.com/JosephSanok

www.pinterest.com/jsanok/angry-kids-frustrated-parents-and-distant-couples-/

www.facebook.com/MentalWellnessParenting

PRIVATE PRACTICE SUBJECTS

Are you a therapist? Check out my blog about everything we should have learned in grad school!

www.PracticeofthePractice.com

www.twitter.com/OfThePractice

Mental Wellness Parenting

MENTALWELLNESSCOUNSELING

Now accepting new clients.

www.MentalWellnessCounseling.com

Thanks for reading, let me know how it goes!

Joe

Action Step List: